A big hug always from me

Date Christmas Day
2007

Dear Fiona
I hope this is not
too "religious" for you,
but remember the
Latin root is 'religio'
which means to bind.
And our bindings are
deep.

much love

From Aunt Lesley

A Hug for You Today

© 2003 Christian Art Gifts, RSA
        Christian Art Gifts Inc., IL, USA

Designed by Christian Art Gifts

Christian Art Gifts has made every effort to trace the ownership of all quotes and poems in this book. In the event of any question that may arise from the use of any quote or poem, we regret any error made and will be pleased to make the necessary correction in future editions of this book.

Unless otherwise stated Scripture taken from the *Holy Bible*, New International Version®. NIV®. Copyright © 1973, 1978, 1984 by International Bible Society. Used by permission of Zondervan Publishing House. All rights reserved.

ISBN 1-86920- 323-2

Printed in China

06   07   08   09   10   11   12   –   10   9   8   7   6   5   4

A Hug for You today

Written and illustrated by
Audrey Jeanne Roberts

christian
art gifts

Dear Reader,

A hug is such a simple act – and yet few things can more powerfully connect us. A hug places us physically heart-to-heart, and even more importantly bonds us together emotionally, heart-to-heart.

This book is full of a variety of hugs. There are some silly hugs and a few profound hugs. Collected like wildflowers along the path of friendship, they've been randomly gathered and tied together in a casual bouquet.

Some of the flowers in this bouquet are tall and stately, others small and cheery or wildly dangling; all have been lovingly sent to remind you how very treasured you are. Sent to brighten your day today, yet they will last to brighten many other days as well.

Audrey Jeanne Roberts

Contents

Hugs are the perfect gift

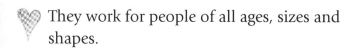 They work for people of all ages, sizes and shapes.

They can be given to family and friends alike.

You can never have too many of them.

They are good for your heart, they are non-fattening.

They are extremely affordable. One-size-fits-all!

A hug a day keeps the blues away.

Hugs are suitable to give for any occasion, but often are considered most valuable when given for no occasion at all.

Hugs are a gift that bring as much joy to the giver as the recipient.

Hugs are the only gifts tha.

Hugs are the only gifts that

10

double in value when they are returned.

double in value when they are returned.

11

A true friend is like a beautiful song, whose melody never fades from your heart.

~ Partraca

A hug says "Hello!"

Whenever we have been apart, whether for a short while or much too long – there is such a joy in our reunion. To see one another and step into each other's arms for a warm and wonderful hug makes the time and distance between us seem to melt away.

For those times when I am not able to wrap my arms around you and give you a giant hug, I'm sending you this book full of a wide assortment of hugs for every occasion and no occasion at all. They are hugs from my heart to yours that I'm sending your way!

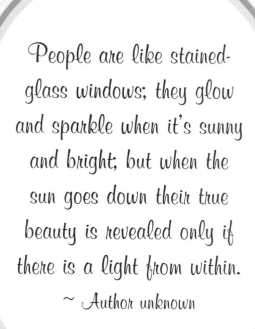

People are like stained-glass windows; they glow and sparkle when it's sunny and bright; but when the sun goes down their true beauty is revealed only if there is a light from within.

~ Author unknown

A hug says, "I appreciate you!"

Sometimes I feel I simply haven't told you often enough how much I appreciate you. I appreciate the warmth of your smile, the gentle touch of your hand as you communicate your compassion. I appreciate all the little things you do and say to make others feel welcome and comfortable.

I appreciate how often you drop whatever you are doing, no matter how important it may be, to be by my side in a time of need. I appreciate you more than it is possible to say in any other language except the language of the heart – given voice through a hug!

Dear friends, let us love one another, for love comes from God. Everyone who loves has been born of God and knows God.

~ 1 John 4:7

A hug is a gift from above

Isn't it amazing how much better we feel after a hug, even if nothing in our circumstances has changed?

Somehow, just knowing we aren't facing things alone and that someone cares, can be enough to encourage us to go on.

God commanded us to love one another and He gave us two arms to do it with! When you give me a hug, I know that you love me and that God loves me too.

A friend is a present
you give yourself.

~ Robert Louis Stevenson

A hug knits hearts together

A hug – four arms wrapped around each other and drawing two hearts together for a moment.

A hug is like a present tied together with a pretty bow – the outside is lovely but the real gift is what's hidden inside.

Friends have their hearts
Joined from the start,
and nothing life brings
can loosen the strings!
~ Audrey Jeanne Roberts

20

$\mathcal{A}$nd let us consider how we may spur one another on toward love and good deeds. Let us not give up meeting together, as some are in the habit of doing, but let us encourage one another – and all the more as you see the Day approaching.

~ Hebrews 10:24-25

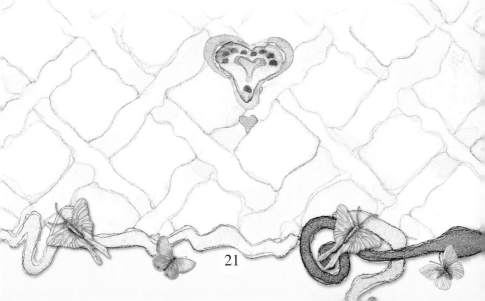

Almost Instantly

As if we'd known each other forever,
we were the

Deepest of friends

Never lacking things to say
or thoughts to share.

Nearly timeless

Even when weeks fly by
and we struggle to stay in touch,
all it takes is a moment and
our hearts are brought together again ...

Almost instantly.

~ Audrey Jeanne Roberts

23

Friends are family
We choose for ourselves!

How great is the love the
Father has lavished on us, that we
should be called children of
God! And that is what we are!
~ 1 John 3:1

Lifelong friendship

From the earliest days of our friendship
we knew it would last a lifetime.
We've walked many different roads together.
At times you've held me up,
other times you've had to lean on me.
Most of the time
we've just enjoyed the view side-by-side.
What a joy it has been to share so many of life's
most memorable moments with someone
as special as you!

A hug says ...
"I'm sorry"

It is not often that we have had differences between us, but when we do, it is comforting to know that the love we have for one another is strong enough to overcome them.

It is amazing how a thick, high wall of ice can begin to melt away with just two simple phrases: "I'm sorry" and "You're forgiven". The last of the ice melts when we reach for each other and embrace in the enveloping warmth of a heartfelt hug.

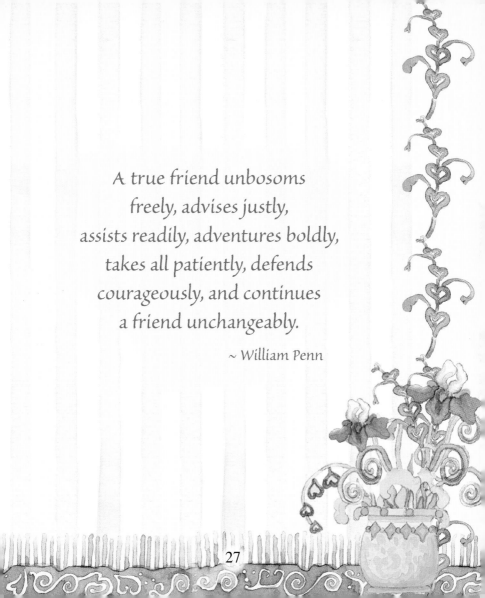

A true friend unbosoms
freely, advises justly,
assists readily, adventures boldly,
takes all patiently, defends
courageously, and continues
a friend unchangeably.

~ William Penn

A hug restores hearts and

renews relationships

We've shared so much laughter,
shared so many tears.
We have a spiritual kinship
that grows stronger each year.
We're not sisters by birth
but we knew from the start
that God put us together
to be sisters by heart.

30

Perfume and incense bring joy to the
heart, and the pleasantness of one's
friend springs from his earnest counsel.

~ Proverbs 27:9

A friend loves at all times, and
a brother is born for adversity.

~ Proverbs 17:17

A hug lends strength

Sometimes when you give me a hug it's as though you pass your strength to me – assuring me that I can face whatever challenge comes my way.

Friendship doubles our strength as we pick each other up when we fall down. We serve each other from a heart of love without thought of reward, rejoicing in each other's accomplishments as though they were our own. We strengthen each other as we pray through each need we face.

One of my greatest joys is to give you in return the very strength you first gave to me – especially when I get to do it through a hug!

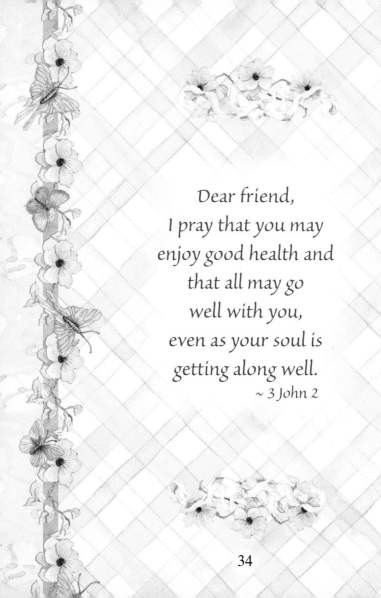

Dear friend,
I pray that you may
enjoy good health and
that all may go
well with you,
even as your soul is
getting along well.
~ 3 John 2

A hug makes you feel better

A hug, a warm blanket and a sweet cup of tea or savory chicken soup – sometimes this is the best recipe for restoring health.

For the times I am not able to be with you at your bedside, I want to send you healing hugs today. A hug to say, "Hang in there, hold tightly to God's promises – trust Him especially when you're feeling down." A hug to say, "I'm praying that your strength will be restored." And a hug to say, "I wish I could make you feel 'all better'!"

Whether we're physically sick, downhearted or perhaps a little of both – a hug brings with it a reminder of God's power to heal.

Two are better than one,
because they have a good return
for their work: If one falls down,
his friend can help him up.
But pity the man who falls
and has no one to help him up!

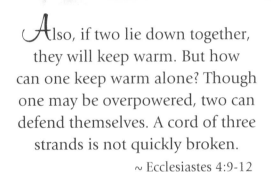

Also, if two lie down together, they will keep warm. But how can one keep warm alone? Though one may be overpowered, two can defend themselves. A cord of three strands is not quickly broken.

~ Ecclesiastes 4:9-12

Friendship consists
of a willing ear,
an understanding heart,
and a helping hand.

~ Frank Tyger

A hug is worth a thousand words

When you are weary and heavily burdened – sometimes I fret that I will not have the right words to say, or even worse I'll say exactly the wrong thing! Though my heart yearns to lift your burden and make everything better, it is rarely in my power to do so.

When words cannot be found and even if they could they would never be enough – I've discovered that a hug is perfect. Speaking more eloquently than a hundred poems or a thousand songs of comfort – a hug gives voice to the universal language of the heart.

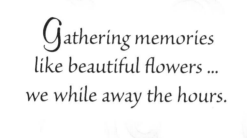

Gathering memories
like beautiful flowers ...
we while away the hours.

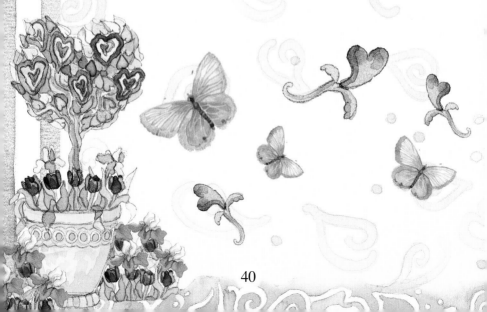

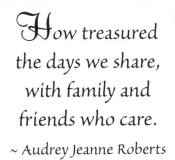

$\mathcal{H}$ow treasured
the days we share,
with family and
friends who care.

~ Audrey Jeanne Roberts

41

Every true friend
is a glimpse of God.

~ Lucy Larcom

A hug of friendship and a chocolate "kiss"

A great friend:

- loves you enough to tell you the truth but is merciful enough not to tell you all of it!

- treasures your best qualities while overlooking your flaws.

- admires your roses, while ignoring your weeds and most importantly ...

- has compassion enough to share her chocolate with you when you are depressed!

We struggle to understand each
other because of the great number
of languages spoken in the world.
But hugs know no language barriers.
Who needs a translator to tell you what
an arm around your shoulders means?

~ Kathleen Keating

Hugs are for "family!"

Sometimes we feel deeply connected to those that are related to us – greeting them with hugs of affection and love. Sometimes family members are so different that were we not bonded by name and family heritage we would find little to draw us together.

Then there are those wonderful people like you, who have shared my life in such a deep way that I've come to think of you as "family!" I can't imagine my life without you being a part of it.

What a miracle – the friendship that becomes even more closely bonded than flesh and blood through the Spirit of God.

A hug is a wish ...

For peace, joy and quietness of heart.

For God's blessings in every area of your life.

For delightful days of sunshine and joy.

For comfort when you feel afraid.

For strength when you grow weary.

For courage when the road you must walk is much longer than you planned.